# MY PERFECT COGNATE

# MY PERFECT COGNATE

Natalie Scenters-Zapico

Copper Canyon Press

PORT TOWNSEND, WASHINGTON

Cover art: María Fragoso Jara, *Cordón umbilical,* 2023.
Colored pencil on paper, 20 × 15.50 in.
Courtesy of the artist and 1969 Gallery (NYC).

Copper Canyon Press is in residence at Fort Worden State Park
in Port Townsend, Washington, under the auspices of Centrum.
Centrum is a gathering place for artists and creative thinkers from
around the world, students of all ages and backgrounds,
and audiences seeking extraordinary cultural enrichment.

LIBRARY OF CONGRESS CATALOGING-IN-PUBLICATION DATA
Names: Scenters-Zapico, Natalie author
Title: My perfect cognate / Natalie Scenters-Zapico.
Description: Port Townsend, Washington : Copper Canyon Press, 2025. |
    In English, with selected poems translated into Spanish. |
    English and Spanish. | Summary: "A collection of poems by Natalie
    Scenters-Zapico"— Provided by publisher.
Identifiers: LCCN 2025022884 (print) | LCCN 2025022885 (ebook) |
    ISBN 9781556597275 paperback | ISBN 9781619323179 epub
Subjects: LCGFT: Poetry
Classification: LCC PS3619.C285 M9 2025 (print) |
    LCC PS3619.C285 (ebook) | DDC 811/.6—dc23/eng/20250610
LC record available at https://lccn.loc.gov/2025022884
LC ebook record available at https://lccn.loc.gov/2025022885

9 8 7 6 5 4 3 2 FIRST PRINTING

COPPER CANYON PRESS
Post Office Box 271
Port Townsend, Washington 98368
www.coppercanyonpress.org

For Ángel, mi amor eterno,
& Jaime, regalo de mis huesos

# CONTENTS

## III

## IV

# MY PERFECT COGNATE

## LANGUAGE ON PAPER

In the beginning was
the Word, & the Word
was with Mother, &
the Word was with Father,
& I learned of violence
through the Word. There
was the Word in Spanish
& there was the Word
in English & at times
they were the same
Word. Other times
the Word did not mean
the same to Mother
as it did to Father.
I never thought to learn
more Words, different
Words from other Mothers,
other Fathers. As a child
I only knew to speak
the family Words. As a child
I saw a stone but did not
think the Word stone.
As a child a stone
was an image made
through fingertips. I write
poems, & each Word
is a little knife I wield
on the page to get back
to the image, the image
of the stone. Am I too
abstract? Perhaps. Still,
can you hear the rain
wash the wild &

brown stone that lives
in the quiet of my mind?
No? I'll try to describe it . . .

In the failure of the Word,
in the buried night, my baby
screams toward the shut door
to get closer to me. I wake
for him. In the failure of the Word,
he screams not knowing the Word
to bring me closer. He screams
& in his screams I understand
he wants—closer. I bring him
to my breast. We get close
to each other without a Word.
With a finger, I wipe his pink gums
& fill him silent. I whisper
in his ear my perfect cognate.
He smiles but does not understand.
Thank God, he does not yet
understand. These Words
of empire are bees in the dry heat
of summer. How they've stung me.
How they sting. How they vibrate
my larynx open. How I thought
I was speaking. How it was
their buzz & amber honey
that moved my body through
this world of Words the whole time.

**I**

*En la noche a tu lado*
*las palabras son claves, son llaves.*
*El deseo de morir es rey.*

*Que tu cuerpo sea siempre*
*un amado espacio de revelaciones.*

*In the night by your side*
*words are codes, are keys.*
*The desire to die is king.*

*May your body always be*
*a beloved space of revelations.*

Alejandra Pizarnik, "Revelaciones"

## FALSO COGNATO

Language is a mirror I never tire of looking into.
Every day I fall headfirst into its red.
Spanish is a trap. English is a diversión.
One makes me the most beautiful woman,
the other tells me to shut my snout, ugly dog.
It's no one's falta I feel regalo in one
& buy my groserías with the other.
English & Spanish hold hands, & ask me
to appreciate them more. I look into language's mirror
for a perfect reflection. I get the cognates right
by getting them all wrong. I'll only buy a mirror
if it makes me skinny-mini. I can't imagine holding
my reflection without making sure it doesn't give me
a jowl. My mind won't stop humming. I blame
all this language I don't know how to speak
running mangled in my head. I'm no villain.
I'm willing to mediate between Spanish & English
so they'll remember, if they ever stop yelling,
that portraits tend to favor the dead.

Lenguaje es un espejo en el que nunca canso de mirarme.
Todos los días caigo de cabeza en su grid.
El español es una trampa. El inglés es una diversion.
Uno me hace la mujer más bella,
el otro me dice que me calle el hocico, perra fea.
No es fault de nadie que me siento regal en una
& compro mis groceries con el otro.
El inglés & el español se toman de la mano & me piden
que los aprecien más. Me miro en el espejo del lenguaje
para un reflejo perfecto. Entiendo bien los cognados
entendiéndolos mal. Solo compraré un espejo
si me pone mini-flaca. No puedo imaginar mirar
a mi reflejo sin asegurarme de que no me de
una papada. Mi mente no deja de tararear. Yo culpo
todo este idioma que no dé hablar
corriendo destrozado en mi cerebro. No soy ningún antagonista.
Estoy dispuesta a mediar entre español & inglés
para que recuerden, cuando paren de gritar,
que los retratos suelen favorecer a los muertos.

## EN COGNATO

Pregnancy turned my thighs into two gray continentes
that rise in the pool. The water's chlorine stench,
an animal with apetito that pushes my shirt against
my chest. I swim with clothes on, afraid my asymmetry
will ofender. My husband likes to touch the indents
on my belly & call them a diamante mine. I have no
interest in being beautiful again. I've given up the magia
of desire for the metal of disgust. I used to think
I was the dictadora of my body, until an army of células
shredded my glándulas to gauze in the ultrasonido's image.
The doctores say I'm excesiva: polyp, cyst, fibroide.
The doctores have to cut the extra of me out. Over the tent
of my body in the operating theater, the doctora asks:
*Did you know you have endometriosis? A constelación*
*of brown in here.* Under the surgeon's lamps I return
to the pool & fill it with cemento. I'm closing down
the horror turístico of my gut. I'm no body of water
but with one swing of my arms I'll break roca
to a cañón large enough to bury the pool,
the yard, & my océano's view of bell-sleeved selves
I've worn in & out of every hamlet & town.

El embarazo convirtió mis nalgas en dos continents grises
que aumentan en la alberca. El hedor de cloro del agua
es un animal con appetite que empuja mi camiseta contra
mi pecho. Nado con ropa puesta, porque tengo miedo de que mi asimetría
pueda offend. A mi esposo le gusta tocar las sangrías
en mi barriga & llamarlos una mina de diamond. No tengo
interés en ser bella otra vez. He abandonado la magic
del deseo para el metal del asco. Antes pensaba
que era la dictator de mi cuerpo, hasta que un ejército de cells
trituraron a mis glands hasta convertirse en gasa en la imagen del ultrasound.
Los doctors dicen que soy excessive: pólipo, quiste, fibroid.
Los doctors tienen que cortar todo lo excesivo de mí. Sobre la tienda
de mi cuerpo en el quirófano, la doctor me pregunta:
*¿Sabías que tienes endometriosis? Una constellation
de café hay aquí.* Debajo de las luces del quirófano regreso
a la alberca & la lleno de cement. Voy a cerrar
el horror tourist de mis tripas. No soy hecha de agua
pero con un movimiento de mis brazos puedo romper rock
hasta crear un canyon tan grande que podre enterrar la alberca,
la yarda, & mi vista del ocean de mis propios seres con mangas acampanadas
que he puesto adentro & afuera de cada aldea & pueblo.

## FALSO COGNATO

I tie a ropa embroidered with medals of pregnant
virgins around my waist. On the shelf
an angel's cheeks swollen red, forever ready to blow
the horno at his lips. In the tin frame above my bed
a pared of saints I leave candles & water for. I hope
each figure leaves me with child. My little cherubs
of delito, I only want to keep you happy. I wash my face
with sopa the color of tar & arrange white-hot
flowers I don't know the name of in a vaso.
I wash my armas in wine to rid myself of salt.
I am trying to be holy & gracioso. I am trying
to become full as a used car lot with a faded sign.
Where is the éxito? I want to recordar this ritual,
so I write it longhand in a bible kept
in my librería of miniature books. Who am I to talk
to God directly? I embroider dark fábrica & ask the saints
to asistir my broken body to have a baby I am told
I want. Do I want it? I do. I do. I do.

Ato un rope bordada con medallas de vírgenes
embarazadas alrededor de mi cintura. En la repisa
las rojas mejillas hinchadas de un ángel siempre listo para soplar
el horn en sus labios. En el cuadro de estaño encima de mi cama
hay una parade de santos a quienes les dejo velas & agua. Deseo
que cada figura me deja con niño. Mis pequeños querubines
de delight, solo quiero mantenerles feliz. Lavo mi cara
con soap el color de alquitrán & coloco flores
blancas-calientes cuyo nombre no sé en un vase.
Lavo mis arms en vino para deshacerme de sal.
Estoy intentando ser santa & gracious. Estoy intentando estar
llena como un lote de autos usados con cartel descolorido.
¿Dónde está el exit? Quiero remember este ritual,
por eso lo escribo a mano en una biblia guardada
en mi library de libros en miniatura. ¿Quién soy yo
para hablar con Dios directamente?
Bordo fabric oscura & pido a los santos
que assist a mi cuerpo roto tener un bebé que dicen
que yo quiero. ¿Lo quiero? Sí. Sí. Sí.

## IN COGNATE

The cognate hides in plain sight.
Little spies everywhere, no sense
without them. Legislation of barbarous
imperialism in dull black ink—the letters
remain the same. It is the order
of letters that renders meaning.
It is the order of letters that renders
the mule deer standing in the desert
from the excavator clearing the desert.
The brain moves somewhere in between
English & Spanish. I say English words
as if in Spanish. I say Spanish words as if
in English. I am looking for slender
& curvaceous spies that carry the keys
to many houses. Some spies are perfect
mirrors that show the body moving across
a tiled hall. Some spies are true mirrors
that show the face refracted, yet whole
& still recognizable. Some spies
are as false as the mirror desilvering
in the bathroom. Who can understand
the cognate except for those who search
for the familiar in the shape
of the foreigner's mouth? A boy is hit
on the head with the bore of a gun.
Out of the boy's head, up in the air,
his cognates float. The boy bleeds
& his cognates do not leave his side.
The cognates must report what is happening
to the boy. Some say they cannot understand
even the most perfect cognate. They cannot
understand the most perfect cognate
if it is pronounced with an accent,

with an accent mark, in an unfamiliar place.
Who am I to translate that which requires
no translation? The cognate is no citizen,
but a cognate will split the land & taint it
black with bollards tall as the letters
in the congressional bill it calls home.
I am trying to better understand why
the cognate is important. It is important
because it is like the coyote in the road—
a trickster, always watching. The cognate
writes its own text, a text only a brain
that breaks English & Spanish can decipher.
I go through the house with a flashlight
searching for the circuit breaker. I find
the circuit breaker hidden in my chest.
Only through the vinegared mirror
can I flip the switches of my chest plate.
Each switch is labeled only in perfect
cognates. The cognates reach out
of my chest, into the mirror, & back
again deep into my throat, which utters:
*Cognato, cognato, cognato.* Do you know
what I mean when I say espejo avinagrado?
Do you know that kind of clean, the smell?
No, you do not know what I mean
because it cannot be expressed in cognates,
it remains stunted in the rock of translation.
Can't you pull every word from the rock
of translation & watch it float to the heaven
of meaning? No, as long as the cognate exists
it will run, tunnel, & swim across languages
to a more perfect meaning. Do not trust
the cognate no matter how identical.

The cognate is not two identical twin bodies.
The cognate is birthed from & gives birth to
one body at odds with the world. I am
a mother who births in lines of cognates.
The men in my family are an afterthought
in their death. What I mean is when the men
in my family throw porcelain dishes on the kitchen
floor we ask: Who is this boy's mother?
The father's agnate only survives in one language.
The mother's cognate is fluent in death & dying.
The cognate knows no bastards. The cognate
knows all her children because she grew them
in her capacious womb. Little boy who dreams
himself king at the tiniest kitchen table,
it is your mother who knows how best to wound
you with her cognate tongue. It is the agnate
that separates, it is the cognate that unifies.
If we built languages in the shape
of our cognate mothers, who would we be?
My wish for my cognate mother is the same
as for my birth mother who calls me crying
on the phone every night. I wish my mother
the bravery to exist beyond her frame of agnates.
Yet, I too, am a mother framed by agnates.
A mother of men who, singular in their meaning,
orbit me. Can you hear my inner cognate whisper
through the mirror's gleam: I require no translation.

## BABY BLUES

Doctors pull a buoyant body from me
& say: *Nurse!* I drape my son across
my plastic-taped incision & let him

grind my nipples with his Epstein pearls.
People ask: *Is it true you couldn't birth*
*your son between your legs in a barn?*

I say: *It hurts between my legs*
*just talking about it.* The moon smiles
a kid-friendly grin & I wonder

which finger Mary used to break
her god's latch. I'm no Mary.
I chose to have a baby

in what my doctor calls a geriatric age.
I chose to have a child the year
the state called me Incubator.

Like Mary I can't stop crying.
My doctor says: *Call this number*
*if you get the baby blues.* I pull

a cartoon smile from ear to ear.
In the dream feed I hear
a navy-blue voice calling,

calling me to drop my tired head.
The voice is blue. It calls blue.
It blue-calls, blue-calls:

*No one wants to read about a mother.*
On a walk with the blue stroller,
a bird calls: *No wants to hear*

*about the mother unless it's from the child.*
I swaddle my son in a blanket so blue
it becomes a river blue unlike

the brown rivers of my childhood.
The brown rivers of my childhood
which swallow mothers & their children

under currents woven in blue blood.
From the blue river I've wrapped
around his infant body, from the streetlights

that tint his room blue, a blue voice
calls me. It calls blue, calls blue:
*Don't write about becoming a mother.*

*Don't write about being a mother.*
*Don't write. Don't write again,*
*you mother—*

## SENTIMENTAL EVENING

The pewter moon's eyebrowed guise
circles a picture of my son. A Windex tear

falls to my son's cheek & I know
we will never fully know one another.

Message after message asking:
*How is the breastfeeding going?*

Let me tell you: *Not great. Not great at all.*
Everywhere advice to make the milk come:

plums, fenugreek, blessed thistle.
This morning each stream of water falling

from my showerhead was a knife ready
to gut me. The pewter moon's smile

wants to eat me whole. Online strangers
tell me to love my postpartum body.

They say: *You are tiger. You are zebra.*
I am desperate to return to the numb feeling

of the surgical theater, the sound
of the doctor mispronouncing my full name.

In the mail a medical bill worth more
than a pickup truck arrives. It arrives before

the state gives my son a social security number,
a birth certificate, a sign of arrival.

Even at my most animal I am the price
of my bearded belly, the price of my crying

breasts, the price of being split,
excavated, vacuumed, & stapled shut.

## MATRESCENCE

I stomp my feet at the Muscovy ducks
that waddle in my path & push my hair

high, high into a yellow claw. I smile
at the high-school boys who throw rocks

at the crib I keep hidden between my eyes.
To the boys, I am just another

absentminded mother. The fathers here
use 20-gauge shotguns to kill the Muscovies,

ducks they say are uglier than sin.
No one would ever guess that like a duck

I bit a man once for sport.
For sport I'd bite a man again

just to feel like the winner. I bit a man for sport
like a father shoots a duck with a shotgun

in the evening rain. Send the fathers out to hunt
me too. Tonight the sky is a hell I long

to plunge into, & Earth is a heaven I hope
to scale like a wall. I chew my loneliness

like a Muscovy duck does a slice of Wonder Bread.
I've tried to die my whole life, but now I rock

the crib between my eyes to feel the pressure
of living. At home I have a child I prayed for, cried for,

went under the knife for & I feel guilty, very guilty,
for being a mother alone on this walk without her son.

# AGNATE

*an interrogation of the* Oxford English
Dictionary

## NOUN

If an agnate is *a relation through the male line,* is this why I used to kiss the
spider-shaped scar on the palm of his hand & say: *Arañita, arañita, ¿cómo
te quiero comer?* & when I felt his arañita against my chest I thought:
*When you love a spider, a spider comes to live inside you.*

## ADJECTIVE

If an agnate is *of or relating to agnates; related through the male line,* is this
why I am ashamed that my father threw the glass just to watch it shatter?
Is this why I am ashamed that my brother punched the door just to watch
it split? Fear of losing my agnate helps me keep the secret. Without an ag-
nate, how will you know what to call me? The Department of Homeland
Security has me listed as Scenters-Zapico de Maldonado, Natalie.

## FIGURATIVE

1.a. If an agnate is *of the same or similar kind, akin, related; having the same
nature,* does this mean that my membranes are stamped with the absence
of my son? Does this mean my brain carries his first feeling? The agnate
wants me to keep everyone I meet full. All around the house there's evi-
dence: We starve.

1.b. If an agnate is . . . *having similar semantic content to another,* then
I will finish this poem with a pair of agnate sentences: I am one of my
father's daughters. My father's daughters are more than me.

## EN COGNATO

I eat cereal from a two-dólar McDonald's glass.
Cadmium-laced red Ronalds dance up & down
to inaudible música. McDonald's will buy
the glass back for three dólares, but why bother?
Ronald, can you find your way to my kitchen?
Or do you need a mapa? The stench of ripe berries
from the refrigerador is comforting. We only eat
orgánico now. In another life someone broke
all my carro's windows, stole a book of cheques,
& spit on the driver's seat. Now I only
have to worry about the shooting up the block
from my house at the Alamo Motel. Now I only
have to worry about someone else's bad life.
What is violencia to me now? Is all this comforting?
I've never felt more uncomfortable in my life. My boss says
she's not my boss—okay, jefa. She calls & calls
at all hours & I automáticamente answer the teléfono
like when I needed horas waiting tables to make renta.
My boss doesn't care about the bebé on my hip,
the pot of broth boiling on the stove. Vapor clouds
my jalousie windows, so I turn a metal knob to let
the vapor from outside cloud them more. This is paraíso:
a home, food in the pantry, a boss who says she's not
my boss, & a bebé crying for more fórmula
I have plenty of. This is paraíso? This is paraíso.
Who knew paraíso was so radiante—so damn bright.

Como cereal de un vaso de McDonald's que cuesta dos dollars.
Rojo Ronalds atados con cadmio bailan arriba & abajo
a music inaudita. McDonald's ofrece comprar
al vaso por tres dollars, pero ¿por qué molestarse?
¿Puedes encontrar como llegar a mi cocina, Ronald?
¿O necesitas un map? El tramo de bayas maduras
del refrigerator es consolador. Ahora solamente comemos
organic. En otra vida alguien rompió
todas las ventanas de mi car, robaron un libro de checks,
& escupieron en el asiento del conductor. Ahora solamente
tengo que preocuparme de la balacera en la otra cuadra
de mi casa en el motel Álamo. Ahora solamente
tengo que preocuparme de la mala vida de los demás.
¿Qué es la violence para mí ahora? ¿Es todo esto reconfortante?
Nunca me he sentida tan incómoda en mi vida. Mi jefa dice
que no es mi jefa—okay, boss. Me llama & me llama
a todas horas & yo automatically contesto el telephone
como cuando necesitaba hours para hacer rent.
A mi jefa no le importa el baby en mi cadera,
la olla hirviendo caldo en la estufa. El vapor nubla
mis ventanas jalousie, por eso doy vuelta a la manilla para dejar
que los nuble todavía más. Esto es paradise:
un hogar, comida en la dispensa, una jefa que dice que no es
mi jefa, & un baby llorando por más formula
la cual tengo mucha más. ¿Esto es paradise? Esto es paradise.
Quien supo que paradise era tan radiant—tan malditamente brillante.

## FALSO COGNATO

This broom of rosemary in my kitchen
declares me empresa. I've lived sin
& sinned, I'm not embarazada
to tell you. My only outings are to visit
the priest sighing in disgust as he raps
his knuckles on the curved wood
in the confessional cabinet. I'm always
trapped in rooms with air-conditioning
& no sun. I roll up the gray carpeta
in my bedroom & beat it in the bathtub.
I only want to turn its gray, white.
*Is this a sin?* I ask the priest. *Depende,*
he replies. Envio anyone who has a friend
they can confess to, & not a priest
coughing through lattice. I want the ritual
of forgiveness, but not the change
of heart rate at being forgiven. I want
the cigarro to take all day, not be inhaled
in two minutes. The dog's blue barco
goes on & on. The dog wants me
to throw a ball I cannot reach over
my pregnant belly. Out of a plastic bag
the grapas roll across my kitchen table.
I cut each one into tiny cubes
for my baby's crab claws. Even the hardest
pan will go soft if you run it under
the kitchen sink & throw it in the oven.
*What ingenuidad!* says the priest.
I tell him, *I'm not empresa for nothing.*

Esta escoba de romero en mi cocina
me declara empress. He vivido without
& he pecado, no estoy embarrassed
a decirles. Solamente salgo de casa a visitar
el cura que suspira en disgusto mientras golpea
sus nudillos en las curvas de madera
del confesional. Siempre estoy
atrapada en habitaciones con aire acondicionado
& sin sol. Enrollo el carpet gris
en mi habitación & la bato en la bañera.
Solamente quiero convertir su gris a blanco.
*¿Es esto un pecado?* pregunto al cura. *Depends,*
el responde. I envy a cualquier persona que tenga un amigo
a quien pueda confesar, & no un cura
tosiendo a través del enrejado. Quiero el ritual
de perdonar, pero no quiero el cambio
de ritmo cardiaco al ser perdonada. Quiero
que el cigar dure todo el día & no poder inhalarlo
en dos minutos. El bark azul del perro
sigue & sigue. El perro quiere
que yo le tiro una pelota que no puedo alcanzar
por encima de mi barriga embarazada. De la bolsa de plástico
las grapes rondan por la mesa de la cocina.
Corto cada una de ellas en cubitos
para las tenazas de cangrejo de mi bebé. Hasta el bread
más duro se volverá blando si la mojas debajo
del fregadero & la tiras en el horno.
*¡Que ingenuity!* dice el cura.
Le digo, *No soy empress por nada.*

## EN COGNATO

My house is a palacio at 1,300 square feet.
*No room for a piano,* said the realtor.
But we make dark música with our feet.
Every year the city is overrun by piratas.
Drunk capitánes wearing tricornios wink at me
from stoplights. The piratas I grew up with
sell fake Fendi in the street. My son waves
at a pirata who wears a flowing blusa over
his chest full of hair. I walk faster & faster.
I've never liked piratas no matter what
they're peddling. Once home, I ladle
limonada into my son's cup with the silicona
straw to protect his bebé gums. We sit
on the brown leather sofá I saved up for
& watch the TV at our feet. My son likes
to trace the shape of the dinosaurio on his shirt.
I don't have the heart to tell him they died out
by asteroide, so I roar & snap my teeth.
Dinosaurios are exóticos, but it's piratas
that will steal your wallet then ask you to buy
a gold dragón escultura that's missing all its teeth.

Mi casa es un palace de 120 metros cuadrados.
*No hay espacio para un piano,* dijo la agenta inmobiliaria.
Pero nos gusta hacer music oscura con nuestros pies.
Cada año la ciudad está invadida por pirates.
Borrachos captains con tricornes puestos me guiñan el ojo
desde los semáforos. Los pirates que yo conocí de niña
venden Fendi falso en las calles. Mi hijo saluda
a un pirate que lleva una blouse fluida sobre
su pecho lleno de pelo. Camino más rápido & más rápido
porque nunca me ha gustado a los pirates no importa lo que estén vendiendo.
Una vez en casa, sirvo lemonade en el vaso de mi hijo
con un popote de silicone para proteger sus encías de baby.
Nos sentamos en el sofa de cuero color café
el que ahorré para comprar & miramos la tele que está a nuestros pies.
A mi hijo le gusta trazar la forma del dinosaur
en su camiseta. No tengo el corazón para decirle
que murieron todos por asteroid, por eso me crujo & chasqueo
los dientes. Dinosaurs son exotic, pero son los pirates
quienes te robarán la cartera & luego te pedirán comprar
una sculpture de dragon de oro a la que le faltan todos los dientes.

# COGNATE

*an interrogation of the* Oxford English Dictionary

### Adjective

1. If a cognate is *descended from a common ancestor; of the same stock or family,* is this why I cling to the worthless ephemera of my abuelita: hairpins, watercolored bookmarks, the plastic jar labeled bicarbonato?

2.a. If cognates are words . . . *descended from the same original language; of the same linguistic family. Of words: coming naturally from the same root, or representing the same original word, with differences due to subsequent phonetic development,* is this why the years of forgetting English is a horizon & Spanish a night? Years of forgetting that language is electricity that pulses down my spine. All language, but no language, makes me a neon-limbed fright.

2.b. If a cognate is *an object of kindred sense or derivation;* spec. *that which may adverbially follow at intransitive verb* . . . is that why I dance a dance—I smile a smile—I laugh a laugh—I live this life—to die this death?

3. If a cognate is *akin in origin; allied in nature, and hence, akin in quality; kindred, related, connected, having affinity,* is this why my son is learning English & Spanish at the same time: *Otro-este-otro-este-otro-este-hi?*

### Noun

1.a. If a cognate is *one related by blood to another; a kinsman;* plural *those descended from the same ancestor, whether through males or females. Thus distinguished from* agnate, *which was limited to* legal *relationship through the father only* . . . is this why my specialty is stripping the mother tongue of taste buds? Like a hot broth, I'll strip any language clean.

1.b. If a cognate is *a relative of a deceased person through the mother,* is this why the mother births & births & births & still with each birth must carry cells in her belly of the child that's left her behind?

1.c. If a cognate is *a relative on the mother's side as opposed to an agnate,* is this why I miss the mother of my childhood? Not the mother who fell down the stairs, who stayed in the US, who survived cancer after cancer after cancer.

2. If a cognate is *a cognate word, term, or thing,* is this why I translate texts from Spanish to English & from English to Spanish, but I refuse to birth them into the world? I keep translations deep in my womb—perhaps forever. I want this world to speak in a molten tongue that burns through all language & leaves behind black volcanic glass.

## PAPER CUTS

While crossing the river of shorn paper,
I forget my name. My body,
a please leave. I want a patron saint

that will hush the dog growling
at trimmed hedges it sees in the night.
I want the world to be without language,

but write my thoughts down just in case.
Send help, the dog's growling
won't let me sleep. I haven't slept in days.

I am looking for a patron saint, but none
will let me pray for guidance. There is a buzz
in my right ear that never goes away, no matter

how hard I hit the side of my head
for loose change. Most mornings I wonder
who I can pray to that will make sure I never

have to survive waking again. Most nights
I forget to pray the rosary, though I sleep with it
by the bed. I don't like TVs because

I'll replay this conversation in my head.
My dead lovers are hungry in the kitchen,
so I fix them food they cannot eat. I make toast

of vellum paper, fry an egg made of crepe. I only want
a patron saint to protect me. From between my legs
I know to birth the baby first, then bleed.

**II**

*Each morning it is her face that replaces the darkness.*
*In me she has drowned a young girl, and in me an old woman*
*Rises toward her day after day, like a terrible fish.*

*Cada mañana es su rostro que reemplaza la oscuridad.*
*En mí ha ahogado a una mujer joven, y en mí una mujer vieja*
*Se eleva hacia ella día tras día como un pez terrible.*

Sylvia Plath, "Mirror"

# WHITE SANDS & THE FLUTE

*Al otro lado del río*
*tengo mi banco de arena*
*donde se sienta mi chata*
*pico de garza morena.*

Mira cómo anda en su banco de arena,
old woman too long drunk. Mira
cómo anda. Look how she drops

a crystal flute to drink from the river.
En su banco de arena, borracha,
mira cómo anda. She looks for herself

in the mirror, shattered blue debris.
She looks for herself in the bloat
of red fish dragged por su banco

de arena. ¡Mira cómo anda, la fea!
Mira cómo anda, la vieja por su banco
de arena. En su banco de arena, mira

cómo anda! The old woman searches
por su banco de arena, for a mountain
covered in trees. Mira cómo anda,

swayed drunk by a reflection of sky—
but where is she? Where is she? She is in
su banco de arena. Mira cómo anda,

mira cómo anda. What was her banco
de arena but a beach missing a sea?
Mira cómo anda. She uses her pico

de garza to needle the breeze. Old woman,
what do you get when you walk from one
banco de arena through the ocean,

to another banco de arena? Only deserts
have viejas that lure women into the sea.
*These white sands drown drunk,* she says.

I listen & know I'll never taste
sand from a desert again. Mira cómo anda,
mi vieja, so far ashore from me.

## THE MIRAGE & THE WALL

A storm grew refracted
beneath our feet. A storm
to break caliche into fine powder.
Caliche's belly made of gravel,
made of sand, made of
clay, made of silt, made of
calcified women who hope
their children will one day roam
the desert floor without a wall,
without a drone, without
fingerprints pressed
into plastic. On an agent's desk,
cards with the biometric details
of women dying of thirst.
Women dying of thirst, not
in deserts but in detention
in the desert where the living
are a little less alive. Isn't it life
that is long, & the living
that is short? To stop the living
we built a wall of steel bollards
& hoped that on the other side
the living would be disappeared
into mirage. A mirage there,
on the other side—not real, not
flesh, but a trick of light, a trick
of heat, a trick of our thirst.
Beyond the wall, we kept building
a wall of shipping containers, a wall
of buoys, a wall to keep the mirages
of people drinking water from
abandoned gallon jugs—out.

The farther away I am from the wall
the more I think of its grated shadows.
Grated shadows that have moved
themselves onto my belly like a semi
B-train with no end in sight.
My body is home to no sea.
No sea for tourists to wander into,
no sea to sink bollards into sand.

# ESPEJISMOS

### Plane

My self-image is best reflected in a white, scratched checkpoint mirror. Tilt your nose left & it moves right. Tilt your hand right & it moves left. *Bang! Bang!* says the plane mirror. *Bang! Bang!* I say back. I fold my fingers into the shape of a gun & blow on the bore like an outlaw. Who has time to look at themselves in a checkpoint mirror? Keep it moving. Shuffle out.

### Convex

I catch strangers as they watch me from my sideview mirror, from my backup camera, from the round acrylic convex mirror that telescopes out of my driver's-side window. I watch the strangers. The strangers watch me. I look the strangers in their convex eyes. I smile into their convex teeth. The strangers catch my body rounded in the corners—they catch me all the same.

### Concave

Like a giant I swing my arms in the concave mirror at the carnival. Like a glutton I pour chips directly into my mouth. Like a clown I laugh as salsa Maggi stains my shirt. Like a protagonist I want to be larger than those around me. Like an antagonist I make it through the checkpoint & enter a new country unbothered. Like a hellcat I feel bigger where the air is polluted. Like a ballbreaker I'm bigger than I seem.

### Non-Reversing

I pinch the corners of my eyes & pull up. I pull the skin around my mouth out. I stretch my jowl toward my ears. I fasten loose skin with a piece of tape. I tease my hair up. I curl my hair down. I brush my make-up on hard. I tell myself: You speak & people can't understand a word you're saying, you dumb pig. My mouth is perfectly reflected in the non-reversing mirror. A non-reversing mirror's nature is true. They say pigs are smart animals. I eat pork nearly every day.

## Two-Way

I assume there's an agent watching behind every mirror. I assume the girl's Hello Kitty compact has a man taking notes on the other side. I assume I'm being watched by anything I can see my face in: the freshly waxed floor, the polished doorknob, the sheen of a sedan. I assume each reflection is a two-way mirror. No two-way mirror makes me act any better than I do on my worst day. I assume my bathroom mirror, that two-way Judas, has an agent on the other side on hold with DHS.

## THE MIRRORS & THE MIRROR

after Rita Dove

| | |
|---|---|
| Plucked hair, | Hair plucked, |
| makes | makes |
| me | me |
| less animal, less man. | man less, animal less. |
| Smooth as | As smooth |
| stone carved toad. | toad carved stone. |
| Bald, small, | Small, bald |
| back nuzzled. | nuzzled back. |
| Luck from birth. | Birth from luck. |
| I have | Have I |
| little hair. | hair little? |
| Lie I still love. | Love, still I lie— |
| Plucked & pluck. | Pluck & plucked. |
| Not once | Once not |
| I felt | felt I |
| pain. | pain. |
| Beautiful: a reflection | Reflection: a beautiful |
| woman hated. | hated woman. |
| I gasp! | Gasp I! |
| Mother dancing | Dancing mother |
| on | on |
| red-lit floors. | floors lit-red. |
| Haggard, old | Old, haggard |
| baby botox brow. | brow botox baby. |
| I love cigarettes, dark lipstick. | Lipstick dark, cigarettes love I— |
| this | this |
| terrible confession: | confession terrible: |

God knows they shaved me
to give birth. God knows I
asked for a mirror to see
between my legs. God
knows I was nowhere in its
reflection. God knows
home has no image we can
agree on. God knows I can't
go home. God knows I am a
home. God knows
motherhood made me home
to my baby's dark hair. God
knows my hair grew back.
God knows I disappear like
home does when waking
from a bad dream. God
knows in the bad dream
mother burns the house
down. God knows who I've
burned. God knows I've
never hurt a soul. God
knows the exception. God
knows I've swallowed lit
matches to see if my
motherhood will catch fire
& smoke up the little blue
house that's my home. God
knows it's my home for
now. God knows it's my
home, for now. God knows
it's only home, for now.

## THE TRICK IS TO PRETEND

the ladder keeps going. The same black dust

that peels the paint off your car

is on each rung. Don't touch your face.

I imagine the police with spotlights,

a system to search my geolocation,

the whir of a drone. I had black lines across

my feet, dark scars. Where did they go?

The game is who can avoid interrogation,

who can split themselves into a hundred

coded squares, lines in alternating

directions going . . . no where. The winner,

who can find the code. I want to enter

this country like the rich with the swipe

of a card, the scan of a face. But they

require my arms, legs, a stomach

strong enough for chemical labor.

I climb knowing the only way down

is by falling. Police paved a concrete

square to catch me, men are waiting

with high-powered hoses to clean me up.

# THE GUN & THE COWBOY

I shoot a piece of paper so pale, from far away, it could be an image of me.
After the range, I search for pills in my desk drawer.
I shake each cylinder swollen with tiny gray beads & imagine falling
    dead-asleep.
I am doing my best not to kill myself before I die.
I do not stay alive for me, I stay alive for you.
I do not want to offend you.
Even in my fantasies I care what you think.
You. You. The all-seeing, eye-snapping performance of you.
*Another day, another victory!*
Or so my therapist says. Would that my mind were as easy to silence as hers.
I'm alive despite the constant pounding in my left ear.
I'm alive unlike the cowboy who shot himself in the middle of a field,
the cowboy who could not stand the ringing in his ears.
Would that I were as brave as that cowboy on a morning such as this.
Another day, I wake to the cruel call of blue jays.
Another day, I rent the gun & do not buy it.
Another day, I read my poems & wonder: *Where is the world?*
Another day, I fall asleep to the dead pounding at my door.
Another day, I cannot find a rock to break.
Another day, I cannot find a break to rock.
Another day, I cannot break these tiny beads into tiny rocks.
Another day, I cannot find. Another day, I cannot.
I cannot. I cannot. I cannot. I cannot. I cannot.

## THE THRONE & CHISPAS

The burning chair in my kitchen
smells nothing like the bonfires
I jumped over in childhood. The bonfires
that once burned the right side

of a boy's face before my eyes,
his eyelashes small traps for bright embers.
We called him Chispas. Chispas! Chispas!
That was the sound of his skin burning

in front of us. The sound of his hair snapping
like hot oil off his face. I wish I could tell you
the burning chair in my kitchen smells
of something deeply archetypal like

sagebrush. But no, it smells like sparks
from the old TV I shot in the desert
with my friend's .45. It felt so good to make
violence & not just watch it. It felt good

to make violence & not just take it.
I am a bad citizen breaking easy laws.
I let the chair in my kitchen burn because
smoke cleanses. One day, I'll wash this char clean.

## THERE ARE WOMEN OUT THERE LIVING

I've met them. God save you
from a woman like me forced

to stay alive. Living makes you
helpless to the yellow tequilita

served in teacups. My mother says
a woman's job is to domesticate.

That's how she keeps a husband
though he likes to disappear

for days. *He'll return,* she says,
*like cattle.* But even cattle need

to be prodded. There are women
out there living. When my husband

wanders into the heat of night,
I don't own a hot stick

to get him back to bed.
There are women out there

living. I park my car deep
in the green heart of this country

& there, hanging from the branches
of a tree, a pair of panties torn

& yellowing in the rain.
Nothing changes. Everywhere I go

I am forced to keep alive. I'd give
my right hand not to end up dead

in a ditch. No one would come
looking for me, this I know.

It's New Year's Day
& there are women out there

living. I keep an extra pair
of panties in my glove box

& remind myself: A rabbit
keeps going. A hawk keeps watch

& hides. In the green heart of this country
I am a woman who knows how to stay alive.

# III

*Yo que sentí el horror de los espejos*
*no sólo ante el cristal impenetrable*
*donde acaba y empieza, inhabitable,*
*un imposible espacio de reflejos . . .*

*I, who felt the horror of mirrors,*
*not only before the impenetrable glass*
*where it ends and begins, inhabitable,*
*an impossible space of reflections . . .*

Jorge Luis Borges, "Espejos"

850  855  860  865  870

I excise the congressional bill
*construction immigration provisions construction*
for cognates & all that remains
*immigration fundamental constitution*
is the violence of abstraction.
*discrimination illegal San Francisco California*
The slurs in H.R. 7059 roar fast:
*illegal federal federal national*
I must remember to slow down
*immigration immigration responsible*
to comprehend the document's lettering:
*illegal criminal MS-13 operations*
I tell the bill I am a heritage speaker
*criminal conviction criminal sexual*
& it foams at the mouth. I am missing
*illegal illegal national immigration visa*
the silent *h*, the accent mark. I invent
*immigration illegal visa illegal*
a word from another etymology.
*immigration mission federal immigration*
I invent a word's context. Do you
*general illegal immigration immigrant*
understand me when I utter:

*provision federal official information immigration*
Can you pick meat off the bones of:
*status status individual individuals*
A broken mind. An incomplete
*federal individuals official information*
articulation. Collapsed English &
*federal officials immigration naturalization*
Spanish mark my heritage tongue,
*eligible immigration national immigration*
mark me diplomat between
*naturalization exception legal political*
my mother's alien tongue &
*political legal political political determination political*
my father's domestic one.
*political determination political construction*
Everywhere I go it is the cognate
*criminal illegal immigrant section general*
shadows that feed the child
*immigration nationality inadmissible immigration*
with one hand & sell the pantry empty
*nationality inadmissible deportable individual*
with the other. I am still searching

47

*official criminal motor individual federal*
for a common language.
*political officials political section color*
Poet, have you found one?
*federal federal civil action political officials*
Maybe it didn't need to be invented
*subdivision official political subdivision*
but detangled from its mother's
*detention detention exception individual*
entrails. I look for familiar
*political subdivision subdivision official*
language in the cognates
*political subdivision political subdivision*
that foam between my legs.
*detention action action individual individual individual*
The foam that announces
*immigration political immigration political*
my body is ready to vacate
*federal political subdivision political subdivision*
the baby. This is the same
*section immigration limitation action action*
foam that forms along the river's
*action subsection detention immigration*

edge. The river whose current
*general section section section detention general*
pushed me down to my cognate
*section section section detention section detention*
mother & carried me up
*general provision section general provision section*
to my agnate father. It is the same
*limitation subsection construction detention detention*
foam that grows along the lip
*detention criminal section conviction alcohol*
of the communion chalice
*inadmissible section deportable via section conviction*
& cleanses the second-language
*attention section immigration exclusion section subsection*
learner's tongue of a childhood
*general ineligible subsection section immigration*
attached to their new tongue.
*conditional section subsection detention immigration*
Can you understand me
*illegal immigration general admission*
when I say:
*admission immigration criminal subsection subsection*

Me entiendes cuando digo:
*admission subsection subsection basis information*
It is the same foam that lives
*admission immigration admission section deportation*
in the corners of the dog's mouth
*reduction section provision section section criminal*
& drops to the dirt that speaks
*criminal official official official admission exclusion*
a language we have yet to fully
*deportation exclusion deportation possession*
understand. At eighteen years old
*immigration organization association commission criminal*
I walked my university campus
*connection identification section section transportation*
& everywhere chalk
*motor section criminal inadmissible criminal*
on concrete, urging anyone
*section criminal illegal criminal deportability section*
who could read:
*immigration criminal deportable criminal*
PROTEST THE BORDER WALL.
*section criminal illegal criminal designation*
So, I went to the protest

*general immigration section designation criminal*
with my sign:
*designation general consultation organization*
JUSTICE SIN FRONTERAS.
*association criminal section notification*
Sin: a false cognate that speaks
*designation subsection communication pro tempore*
to the sin I was about to see
*organization association basis publication federal*
built in the bundles of rust rods,
*designation federal notification general*
strewn like bars to a cell
*designation subsection information information*
the State was making of our desert.
*Designation subsection information information*
No cameras, no journalists, no
*ex parte camera subsection subsection information*
professors at the protest. Only
*information ex parte camera subsection*
a group of students run off
*designation general designation subsection*
by bulldozing equipment &

*subsection designation petition general*

985

border patrol. Only little boys

*designation criminal designation club organization*

kicking a soccer ball two by two.

*association petition revocation petition club*

Can you understand me:

990

*organization association petition revocation*

Me entiendes cuando te digo:

*petition designation designated club organization*

If a protest happens & no one

*association petition association petition revocation*

is there to document it, a poem

995

*petition determination petition club organization*

will show the protest happened.

*association petition revocation designation*

Understand:

*criminal petition section determination general*

1000

Entiendes:

*petition revocation determination revocation*

Fifteen years later the president

*information determination petition revocation*

who promised not to build

1005

*information information ex parte camera*

52

any more wall announced today

*information ex parte camera subsection publication*

he would continue to build

*determination determination federal revocation* ——————

more wall. I want the cognates

*designation general designation criminal designation*

to prove we have some common

*petition revocation applicable publication*

understanding. I dream ——————

*federal revocation designation revocation general*

a cognate so perfect it is

*designation club organization association designated*

a bridge to meaning ——————

*criminal section national revocation evocation*

something to each other

*revocation revocation*

through sound. Me entiendes:

*publication federal revocation revocation designation*

Understand me: ——————

*action*

I have spent the last nine months

*revocation designation designation subsection*

erasing H.R. 7059 while a baby

*designation designation general designation subsection*

grows inside of me. A baby

*club organization association alias*

I made with the man I fell

*club organization association designation*

in love with despite the State

*federal subsection designation information information*

trying to arrest me for it. A baby

*information designation subsection information*

made of me, a woman, who

*information ex parte in camera subsection section*

has given Homeland Security

*designation general publication federal designation*

more of herself than she'd ever

*designation determination petition revocation*

write in a poem. I am trying

*designation club organization association*

to create an erasure of H.R. 7059

*basis subsection ex parte in camera information*

while a baby grows inside

*designation designation determination petition revocation*

1055        1060        1065        1070

of me, but what good is erasing
*designation designation determination petition*
words that create physical
*revocation limitation substantial information*
violence against bodies
*action designation designation determination revocation*
& bodies
*application section final designation designation*
of people & bodies
*determination petition revocation section information*
of land? I ask myself
*national national consultation section detention*
over every page: Who is
*criminal general section immigration inadmissible*
the cognate's mother? Who is she?
*section deportable section annual consultation*
During my last month of pregnancy
*federal committees restriction section immigration*
I leave the erasure in the dining room
*section section section section section section*
carefully wrapped in kitchen twine
*subsection section provision visas section*
I used to tie a turkey's legs. I go

*immigration section section immigration section*
to the hospital. Doctors cut
*immigration subsection section criminal*
my baby from me. I come home
*section provision construction subsections*
from my butchering & can't keep
*residential general subsection general*
erasing. In toner the cognates
*general limitation provision notification*
watch me. Quieres oír
*subsection notification justification*
como murmuran los cognatos:
*subsection subsection section*
Do you want to hear
*construction section provision*
how the cognates murmur:
*subsection section*
Quieres entenderlas:
*control control*
Do you want to understand them:
*exclusion section*

# IV

*In a physical world, the mirror is a slice*
*of dark space. How do you break a space? No.*
*Tell me a story set in a different time,*
*in a different place. Because I am scared.*
*I'm scared of the child I'm making.*

*En un mundo material, el espejo es una porción*
*de espacio oscuro. ¿Cómo se rompe un espacio? No.*
*Cuéntame una historia ambientada en una época*
*diferente, en un lugar diferente. Porque tengo miedo.*
*Tengo miedo del niño que estoy creando.*

Bhanu Kapil, *Humanimal*

# 1,723 MILES AWAY FROM HOME

For years, doctors wrote in private files
of my paranoia, my panic disorders. I took
slow-release pills that made me start a story,

then laugh: *I just told you this one, didn't I?*
Strangers would roll their eyes. But I was well-liked
& enjoyed holding company with the living.

I would wake up & count the hours until
I could return to bed. I suffered an illness caused
by the sun on my neck. A shrill opera of summer insects

made me want to be a mother like the mother I had—
a mother who wouldn't get out of bed.
At dinner parties people would look for signs

of my poverty when I'd tell them I got married
at twenty-three on a hot day in June.
How to explain that the state has my whole life

documented in interrogations, home visits, photographs,
medical examinations, tax records, family history,
a bankroll of debt. Five years of humiliation

for a green card to arrive in an unmarked envelope.
A green card—not mine.
A green card for the man I love.

Couldn't I swap out the numbers, the photo, the name,
each chipped facial scan for every person
who needed one? I could not,

but I imagined. I gave myself away
again & again. The girl dancing cumbia in the kitchen
never returned. No community would have me,

so I communed with the spoonful of bad medicine
under my tongue. After a reading to a full auditorium,
a woman nagged me through a microphone:

*Tell the youth in this room what you do for self-care.*
I told her: *I spend long periods in silence*
*which help me survive another year.*

Like most people, I fear dying.
Like most people, I fear dying
far from home.

# THESE RIVERS, THE UNITED STATES, & ME

In ALABAMA I ran across a park so green: the trees green, the sky green, the river green, the houses green, & the little dog barked a green mean thing.

In ALASKA, during the anxious hour when the cat screamed from my broken window, I imagined my body a sheet of ice floating in a flooded river.

In ARIZONA I jumped from rock to rock & fell on a barrel cactus. My hands two blood moons. Each needle a hook to catch fish. The river nowhere to be found.

In ARKANSAS I cried to feed the river. I cut my tears into tiny pieces for the river's pincer grasp, in strips for the river's palmar grab. I cut my tears to feed the river who moved his head away: *Yuck!*

In CALIFORNIA I watched my mother's hair fall out. Her eyes ran dark-river currents to her chest. Her nails were scorpions that glowed blue against white bedding. The radio played a tune about sex that made me want to break the speaker with my fist.

In COLORADO I rode a river brown as clay in the blow-up kayak. When the kayak popped I rode the river on my hands and knees lifting pebbles covered in worms.

In CONNECTICUT I dropped brie on the parquet at the reading. I was the only one invited to dinner who had not graduated from an Ivy League. I spilled red wine on a white tablecloth & joked: *It was a glass, not a river!*

In DELAWARE a man moved a river in a painting that hung over my bed. Or did a man wade through a river in a painting that hung over my bed? I spent the night with many men & many rivers in paintings that hung around my bed.

In FLORIDA the river, the sea, & every bar glowed a cheap iridescent blue. Every day I drove by a motel where a bouquet of blue plastic roses hung tired. Blue plastic roses to remember those who died in a shooting. Above us all a billboard with a handgun—a gun show was coming to town.

In GEORGIA I stood on the lip of a stage & read poems about a man who loved me so much he tried to kill me & then was disappeared. I read poems about the river that witnessed it all. After, a woman told me, *I feel sorry for you.* I bled through my skirt in the back of the Lyft.

In HAWAII there's a conservancy where poets are invited to plant palm trees. I wonder if I will ever write poems that will plant palm trees. I wonder what color the rivers are in a place with native palm trees. I wonder a river.

In IDAHO I made love under the buzz of fluorescent motel lights. From the window a river called my name, but I did not leave those starchy sheets to answer. If a life without water is death, I wanted it.

In ILLINOIS the streets were covered in mirrors made of a frozen river's gasp. Two of me everywhere, I smiled so hard my jaw sprained.

In INDIANA I counted the barns, the silos, the little brown sheds that sat in fields. I looked for water. I looked for rivers. I looked for the sea.

In IOWA the novelist said he was searching for a river. The novelist said he was searching for the river between a woman's legs. His teeth shone gold by candlelight.

In KANSAS there are rivers made of rain, made of drainage, made of fecal coliform. There are rivers made of water you cannot graze with a five-fingered glove.

In KENTUCKY I was a good American woman and watched as a man slapped his wife at the state fair. A river of people parted around them.

In LOUISIANA I got drunk on moonlight & danced with my suegra. She apologized & I apologized. Our feet brought clouds down to earth in the river's bank.

In MAINE I caught a trout & took it home. I kept the fish in the fridge for days. I enjoyed the stench, the blood-brown eyes, the dark river it leaked on the clear plastic shelf.

In MARYLAND I rode a bus through strip malls that could have been anywhere in America: Target, Tuesday Morning, Bed Bath & Beyond. There was a river somewhere, but what discount could a river offer me?

In MASSACHUSETTS I refused to leave the hotel room for the reading. I curled up in bed. I dimmed the lights & closed the curtains. I rocked myself shut & breathed into a paper bag. I wanted the ecstasy of drowning in my riverbed.

In MICHIGAN I was all quiet. My body was all snow. My body was all small, all melt, all river.

In MINNESOTA I became desperate as a dog. I hid my book in an editor's coat pocket. Desperate as a dog looking for water I drank from the river, I drank from the creek.

In MISSISSIPPI the cicadas followed me everywhere I went like a madman's chime. I asked for strong liquor, a river to drown. I asked for a gun, & when I got neither I packed my bags & went on the run.

In MISSOURI the mentor took me out to eat. She read me poems. She told me stories. The mentor appears wherever a river has been moved, dried, dammed. This poem has been moved, dried, dammed.

In MONTANA a stranger told me about a river that would cure me. I went to the river that would cure me. I drank from the river that would cure me & said: *I am cured!*

In NEBRASKA I counted calories as a last-ditch effort to stay twenty-three-thin. But thirty had already hit hard, so I ran by the river & swatted at fleas in low grasses.

In NEVADA I played corridos on the bar's jukebox. I sang about a river that broke my life. Give me a few drinks & I forget northern etiquette. The bartender cut the music & asked me to leave.

In NEW HAMPSHIRE I reread this poem from beginning to end in the empty hotel room. The ceiling opened & a river poured over me.

In NEW JERSEY there was a blackout. Without electricity, I walked the streets in erasure. A roar from the river churned the lights back on.

In NEW MEXICO I cleared the park of the addict's needles before marrying my husband in my makeshift gown. I made friends with the women who worked my street corner. I watched a man drink a bottle of mouthwash & piss a river for scrub.

In NEW YORK they imported me as an artist for the weekend. Everywhere I went artists asked me when I had done my New York years. I treat New York like water does the rivers that flow through Manhattan. I visit & clamor, then leave.

In NORTH CAROLINA I sat in one corner of the living room, the TV in the other. The news was talking ugly about El Paso again. I became suspended in a river of electricity. Poetry had taken me far, far away into this America, these United States.

In NORTH DAKOTA I scraped tar off my shoe & spit tobacco in the dirt. I imagined a horse so thirsty that when it found a river, it drank until its belly burst. My therapist asked if I'd had any suicidal ideation. I always answer the same: *No.*

In OHIO I stayed in every bed & breakfast the state offered. Over scones & black coffee, I was asked by innkeeper after innkeeper if I knew any narcos. Once I was asked: *Do people really cross the Rio Grand in shorts come winter?*

In OKLAHOMA I became a river in need of a dirt cradle. I needed dirt to cradle all the water that was boiling inside me. I bailed my body of water with a spoon.

In OREGON I wet my birth certificate, my passport, my social security card. I wet the water bill, the food-store coupons, the maps I used to find my way to rivers I could wet. Waist-deep I wet.

In PENNSYLVANIA I wanted art to heal me. I ran my fingers across a river in a canvas. The river was dry, just like the river back home.

In RHODE ISLAND I cried when the baby cried. I cried & cried & cried & cried. A river is a mother that pushes her children downstream.

In SOUTH CAROLINA, ounce by ounce, I drank any old thing the dark-haired bartenders put in front of me. I wanted to be baptized in their river. I didn't want to die, but I wanted my crown of thorns bloody.

In SOUTH DAKOTA my thirst consumed me. My eyes flaked & peeled . . . I wanted water. I found a river but could not bring myself to drink.

In TENNESSEE a woman asked why I was still wearing a mask. She asked if there was a new virus going around that she didn't know about. I told her: *I'm still wearing a mask because I'm ugly.* I found a river & drank it dry.

In TEXAS I only wanted to go home. I went to the river that raised me, the bars that drank me, the mountains that grazed me. Everywhere I went people told me I was a stranger. I cried tears no one wants to hear about.

In UTAH I searched the men I met for rivers that had gone missing. I traced each man's tattoo of a coyote, each tattoo of red rocks. How does a river go missing?

In VERMONT I imagined the snow a river come down to drown me. I repeated: *Today, Natalie killed herself . . . Today, Natalie shot herself . . . Today* . . . I took pills filled with tiny spheres. I moved across my kitchen counter like mercury in a shattered thermometer.

In VIRGINIA I lit a candle to San Judas & said I'd cut my hair off if he granted me peace. The next day, I went to the river to find peace. I could not stop crying. In Virginia San Judas shunned me. In Virginia I kept my hair long.

In WASHINGTON I scowled at beautiful women. I barked at ugly men. I wanted a river in my lover's eyes. I was water witch. I was neon devil.

In WEST VIRGINIA I saw an exhibit on clogging. I was a foreigner in a foreign land. Was this not part of my country too? I swam in a river. I felt no connection.

In WISCONSIN my father was raised. His stories are all Americana: backyards & sidewalks & fourth of July. His stories are all Americana: the girl who stabbed her teacher, the man who drowned his wife in a river in front of their kids, the flasher at the playground near school.

In WYOMING I was afraid of the poem. I was afraid of writing a poem. What would my son think of the pain of his mother? What use had I for poetry that did not risk falling off a creased cliff? I found a river & wrote to it. From the current, the poems returned.

## OBJECT MOTHER

At the Vintage Car Wash I keep guard over the flat-screen TV hung in a corner of the concrete waiting room. I watch live video footage of my car being pulled by conveyor belt through a tunnel. I watch as rotating arms punctured with hoses spray the car pink, blue, yellow, then technicolor. The car moves through the tunnel real slow & I already miss my car like I'd miss a womb upon leaving it. My car leaves the flat-screen TV & from the glass doors of the car wash I watch two men in red polos drive it around the side of the building to shammy dry. I exit the building to be reunited with my car, to be given the keys, to leave a tip, to return to my womb, to drive home. I exit the concrete waiting room but cannot find my car, so I wait for it like a child lost in a shopping mall. I ask strangers: *Have you seen my mother? Have you seen my womb?* No, the strangers have not seen my mother, they have not seen my womb, nor have they seen my car. I go back inside & frantically ask the attendant: *Have you seen my mother? She is green. She is a car, too big to miss.* The attendant rolls footage of my car going through the tunnel, then surveillance where two men in polos like those of the men who work at the car wash get in my car, get in my womb, its key in the engine, & drive off. The attendant says: *Probably gone to Mexico by now, probably stripping it for parts, probably burning off the VIN as we speak, probably be used to transport drugs now, probably never gonna see it again.* I am frantic. I am in tears: *I'm never gonna see my mother again?* The attendant says: *Oh baby, you'll see your mother again. Just not in the United States.*

## PLEDGE ALLEGIANCE

I tap-tap-tap the window, while my mother smiles & mouths,
*Tranquila.* I tap-tap the glass, my mother a fish I'm trying to summon.

I tap until a border agent says: *Stop.* Until a border agent
shows me the gun on her belt. I thought myself a movie star

blowing kisses at the children selling Chiclets on the bridge.
My cruelty from the backseat window caught on video—

proof I am an American. My childhood was caught on videos
border agents deleted every three months. The drug-sniffing

dogs snap their teeth at my mother detained for her thick accent,
a warp in her green card. My mother who mouths, *Tranquila.*

My mother's fingers dark towers on a screen for the bioten scan.
*Isn't it fun?* says the border agent. The state takes a picture

of my mother's left ear. *Isn't it fun?* I tap-tap-tap the glass
& imagine it shatters into shiny marbles. A marble like the one

I have in my pocket, the one I squeeze so hard I hope to reach
its blue swirls. Blue swirls I wish were water I could bring to my mother

in a glass to be near her. Friends, Americans, countrymen, lend me your ears!
But only the border agent replies, *Do you know the Pledge of Allegiance?*

She points to a flag pinned on a wall. I do, so I stand & pledge to the country
that says it loves me so much, it loves me so much it wants to take

my mother far away from me. Far away, to the place they keep
all the other mothers to sleep on rubber mats & drink from rubber hoses.

*Don't worry,* says the border agent, *we will take good care of your mommy.*
My mother mouths, *Tranquila.* Her teeth, two rows of gold I could pawn

for something shiny, something shiny like the border agent's gun.
Friends, Americans, countrymen, lend me your ears, so I can hear

my mother through bulletproof glass, so I can hear her over the roar
of American cars crossing this dead river by the wave of an agent's pale hand.

## SMALL UNMANNED AIRCRAFT SYSTEMS

With the swivel of a controller
an agent in a room of laced
concrete blocks is haunted
by bovine hitting their bulk

against steel bollards.
Lidar: Pulsed light shot
from miles overhead
to capture the mundane.

It's true, a man
is haunted by bovine
through a screen & laughs
at his own haunting.

Most lidar paints a picture
in fluorescence of animals
roaming. The agent
is in a city faraway

from all he surveils. He sings
to the pinks, blues, & greens
on his screen: *Oh give me a home*
*where the bovine do roam*

*& the skies are not*
*cloudy all day.* The agent
enjoys days like this, when
the desert is a congress

of ghosts on a screen
not a diaspora of men
& women filled
with thirst. *The red man*

*was pressed from this part*
*of the West, it's not likely*
*he'll ever return.* The agent
opens a bottle of water

& takes a long drink.
*Where seldom is heard*
*a discouraging word*
*& the skies are not*

*cloudy all day.* The agent
throws the half-empty bottle
in a plastic-lined trash can.
He glides his sUAS down

the edge of his assigned piece
of geofencing & breaks the screen
with a pixelated image of a palo verde
that spans the width of the sun.

## AGENT

*an interrogation of the* Oxford English Dictionary

1.a. If an agent is *a person who or thing which acts upon someone or something,* then could the agent serve as a welcome: a hand, a house, a door to a room with a bed & running water? If an agent is *one who or that which exerts power; the doer of an action,* then could the agent release the detainees? Could the agent take a baseball bat to the surveillance camera? Does the agent have agency?

1.b. If an agent is *a person or thing that operates in a particular direction, or produces a specified effect,* then could an agent serve as a boat, a ride, a guide from one country to another?

1.c. If an agent is *the doer of an action, typically expressed as the subject of an active verb or in a* by-*phrase with a passive verb,* then could I erase the agent by writing, "A boy walking in the desert," instead of what is printed in the newspaper, "A boy walking in the desert is apprehended by CBP agent"?

1.d. If an agent is, as *in telepathy: the person who originates an impression* (*opposed to the* percipient *who receives it*), then can I fly a small drone to the other side of this life? Can I leave my body in the room that maneuvers the controller? Can I return to my dead family, though they are not buried in one singular land?

2. If an agent is *a person acting on behalf of another,* can I hire a personal agent to talk to this CBP agent & tell him he should wave all these cars through this checkpoint?

2.a. If an agent is *a person who acts as a substitute for another; one who undertakes negotiations or transactions on behalf of a superior, employer, or principal; a deputy, steward, representative,* then can I please speak to your supervisor? & by supervisor, I mean the President of the United States.

2.b. If an agent is *a person or company that provides a particular service, typically one that involves arranging transactions between two other parties,* then what is the difference between the agent & the trafficker? Los dos venderían a su propia madre.

2.c. If an agent is *an official appointed to represent the government in dealing with an Indigenous people,* then why must the Bureau of Indian Affairs continue to capture CCTV of all Indigenous American peoples?

2.d. If an agent is *a person who works secretly to obtain information for a government or other official body; a spy,* then can one be an agent without also being a peeping Tom, a voyeur, a perverse man behind a screen in a concrete room in a city far away?

2.e. If an agent is *a person who negotiates and manages business, financial, publicity, or contractual matters for an actor, performer, writer, etc.,* then as a poet could I hire an agent to make a contract with my body to return to who I was before I ran my car off the road during a panic attack from which I never fully recovered?

2.f. If an agent is *a stagecoach robber,* then can I rally a group of like-minded bandits to stone the drone, demolish the surveillance tower, shoot the satellite, tear down the virtual border wall?

3. If an agent is *the means by which something is done; the material cause or instrument through which an effect is produced,* then can the agent unfurl their tongue to speak of the horrors they work to create at the bridge, the interrogation room, the transport bus, the detention center?

4. If an agent is *a substance that brings about a chemical or physical effect or causes a chemical reaction,* then the CBP agent corrodes the border as hydrogen peroxide corrodes a metal pipe.

5. If an agent is *a program that (autonomously) performs a task such as information retrieval or processing on behalf of a client or user,* then may all agents show generous agency—a hot meal, a gallon of water, a child never taken to a van on a day that reads 104 degrees.

## PRESENT THIS RECEIPT TO CBP

At the passport scanner
an X tells me I must go
to an agent for further
questions. My mother
has been pulled aside by
uniformed men & placed
in glass-walled offices
my entire life, but I have never
been selected. The agent
asks: *Why were you away*
*so long?* I have been trained
by my mother how to answer
agents my entire life, so I
reply: *Oh, just visiting,*
*Sir.* I smile. I smile so hard
my jaw quivers. As the agent taps
my American passport on the
counter I am comforted by my
citizenship, just as I've been
discomforted by mother's lack
thereof. The agent tells me
I have been pulled from
the line because I travel
so often to Mexico that I should
get Global Entry. The agent
says: *With Global Entry you*
*can come & go as you*
*please. No more lines, no more*
*wait.* I think of my mother
who has stopped traveling
because she's tired of being
pulled from lines despite
her green card. I look at my

hands & reply: *Oh yes, yes*
*I will look into that.* The agent
returns my passport. The linoleum
floors glare bright & I imagine
my mother in an office somewhere—
they will not let her leave. I go
home. I pour myself a glass
of water & look up Global Entry
online. I do not apply, instead
I call my mother & tell her
this story. My mother asks: *Did you*
*smile the whole time? Yes,*
I say, *I smiled the whole time.*

## THE AERYON R80D SKYRAIDER

bobs against waves
of heat that emanate
from the pavement. The sUAS
finds a rattlesnake & scans

its face for recognition. Audio
of a rock falling, radar of a rock
falling, seismic footage of a rock
falling, acoustic vibrations

of a rock falling, magnetic
gauss of a rock falling—
here even the rocks
must show documents that they are

matter. The sheep are atoms
that drift across a screen
to an agent in a concrete room
in a city far away. The agent

& his SkyRaider work to vacate
the land. The agent says:
*This is the way it's supposed to be.*
*I work to make it the way it once was.*

The desert has never been
as the agent imagines it. Each day
the agent works to make the desert
an absence the size of an ocean.

The desert held the ocean once
& will hold it again:
*The way it's supposed to be,*
*the way it once was.*

## DRONE

*an interrogation of* the Oxford English Dictionary

1. If a drone is *a male bee in a colony of honeybees or other social bees,* then are all males part drone—searching, always searching to inseminate the queen?

2.a. If a drone is *a person who does little or no useful work, or who lives off others; a lazy person,* then to be a drone is the greatest insult in America. The crime of living not to produce honey but to enjoy it over toast.

2.b. If a drone is *a person who is engaged in, or made to do, dull, repetitive, or meaningless work,* then I drone at the kitchen table daily: fork to plate to mouth to plate to mouth to plate to sink.

3.a. If a drone is *a remotely piloted or autonomous unmanned aircraft, typically used for military reconnaissance or air strikes,* then can I send a bee-drone to inspect the perimeter unhindered by man's great abstract military equipment?

3.b. If a drone is *a remote-controlled or autonomous vehicle or robotic device which operates in an environment or setting too dangerous or difficult for a human operator to work in, such as underwater, underground, on another planet, etc.,* then how can drones be used where I played hide & seek in the desert with my brother & sister? Were we children underwater? Children underground? Children on another planet? Children of drones?

3.c. If a drone is *a small remote-controlled flying device, typically a small four-rotored helicopter, which has a relatively short range and which is typically used for commercial, recreational, and other civilian pursuits, esp. aerial photography,* then from this far above the whole city becomes a vacant lot—each street a cabled ribbon of trash, each body a bee in search of water, in search of a hive demolished without warning from a cloud above.

# CCTV

after Federico García Lorca's
"La cogida y la muerte"

The wind on the ears of a cottontail
on video-capture at five in the afternoon,
a rat snake undulates through dirt
on video-capture at five in the afternoon,
a mule deer eats tender shoots
on video-capture at five in the afternoon,
a pronghorn bucks, he bucks
on video-capture at five in the afternoon,
a wolf nips the legs of a sheep
on video-capture at five in the afternoon,
a kit fox disappears into the brush
on video-capture at five in the afternoon,
two neon eyes blink in the shade
on video-capture at five in the afternoon,
a roadrunner weaves through mounds of dirt
on video-capture at five in the afternoon,
a falcon hooks his talons on a steel bollard
on video-capture at five in the afternoon,
a man covers his face with a rag
on video-capture at five in the afternoon,
a woman cuts a round into a saguaro
on video-capture at five in the afternoon,
a girl twists her ankle on a rock
on video-capture at five in the afternoon,
at five in the afternoon.
At five in the afternoon.
Every living thing is on video-capture,
an apparition to a man
in a concrete room in a city far away
at five on the dot in the afternoon.

## I WANT DRONE FOOTAGE

of my face as a mother. I want the undulating
landscape of my profile gigantic as the curves

of a desert I can only grasp when caught
from far away. I want the wrinkles under my chin,

the purple rings under each eye to make sense
only at great heights. I want drone footage

of myself as a mother tired from caring
for my newborn son projected onto a wall

to an audience of fathers who tell one another
what great fathers they are. The fathers love

telling one another they do all the cooking,
they are in charge of bath time, they

are nothing like their fathers. They are an audience
of great fathers come to watch me, a terrible

mother whose face only makes sense at great heights.
A terrible mother who slept well past her shift at work,

past her shift with the baby, so that a drone
could make sense of her face from an unnatural height.

The fathers all got an evening off from being
great fathers. Their babies are all at home

with mothers no one, not even
the drones, can find.

is all I ask for. A glint of copper wire
for tummy-time. I want to have a baby,
but I want the baby to be all mine.
Can a human being ever belong
to another human being? Perhaps,
if only for a time. Belong. I belonged
nowhere & I wanted company
in the flicker of night. When I'm home
sick I pull up live video footage
of people crossing the Santa Fe bridge
by foot: a man in a Dodgers hat,
a woman dressed up & down
in the interlocking *G*s of Gucci,
the flash of a girl's bright-blue
hair. How easy it is to give in to one's
nostalgia. How quickly I become
no different than the border agent
in a concrete room, in a city far away,
who watches strangers cross from one
country to the next. What I wouldn't give
to be a stranger. But nostalgia makes us
surveillers of all we want & cannot have,
of all we had & lost. Today I lost
a baby. I hold the pain, a cold jagged stone
under my tongue. I delete my longing
for the nest, the copper wire—I do not
mourn. What right did I have to yet another
human being? Maybe the child was always
a longing in my mind. I zoom in
on strangers crossing the bridge.
Their pixelated faces, abstractions
of the people they are in real time.

What right did I have to mother yet another
human being? The loss of this little
never-was or would-be—my body's failure
to carry—a perfect cognate in my mind.

## NOTES

All translations of section epigraphs are my own.

All poems titled "Falso Cognato" use false cognates in the first stanza on one page & what they sound like they would mean in "correct" Spanish on the next page.

All poems titled "En Cognato" use both perfect & true cognates in the first stanza on one page & the "correct" English translation of those words in the Spanish translation on the next page.

All poems titled "Falso Cognato" & "En Cognato" are imperfect reflections of one another & should be read for many meanings across languages.

The poem "En Cognato" on page 22 references the cadmium-painted glasses that were widely sold at McDonald's restaurants during my childhood.

The poem "En Cognato" on page 26 references the Gasparilla Pirate Fest in Tampa, Florida.

All "mistranslations" in these poems should be read as purposeful.

The poems "Agnate," "Cognate," "Agent," & "Drone" all use definitions from the *Oxford English Dictionary* in italics.

"White Sands & the Flute" begins with a rhyme recited often for the lotería card "La Garza."

"The Gun & the Cowboy" references Texas Roadhouse founder Kent Taylor who killed himself after struggling with a ringing in his ears due to post-COVID symptoms.

All italicized lines in "H.R. 7059 in Cognates" are made up of both the perfect & true cognates found in H.R. 7059, otherwise known as the "Build the Wall, Enforce the Law Act of 2018." The numbered lines in the poem mark the number line in the book up to that point & reflect the numbered metal poles that label parts of the border wall. These numbers are often used by CBP to designate & assign areas of land for surveillance. My goal was to have a conversation, an argument, with the text of H.R. 7059, & in doing so attempt to poke holes & build bridges with cognates (some real, some failed, some false) in this specific discursive landscape that is both very real & imagined.

"Small Unmanned Aircraft Systems" uses the lyrics to "Home on the Range," also known as "My Western Home," by Dr. Brewster M. Higley (1871). The original song lyrics reference "buffalo," which I changed to "bovine" because cows are much more common in surveillance drone footage than buffalo or bison.

"A Tiny Nest of Paper" references the live CCTV footage that anyone can readily access online to watch people cross the border in real time.

## ACKNOWLEDGMENTS

Thank you to the following publications where sometimes earlier versions of these poems appeared: *32 Poems;* Academy of American Poets Poem-a-Day; *Copper Nickel; Florida Humanities: Climate Crisis Folio; The Georgia Review; Gulf Coast; The Kenyon Review; Meridian; Narrative; New England Review; The New Republic; The Paris Review; Puerto del Sol; Southern Indiana Review;* & *The Yale Review.*

"Sentimental Evening" was republished in *Best American Poetry 2024* & in *The Washington Post.*

This book was written in the quiet of a depression that lasted several years. I could not have seen my way out of it without the help of the love of my life, José Ángel Maldonado. Mi amor, the best part of the pandemic was falling in love with you all over again. Thank you to our son who made me a mother & reminds me to laugh more. Thank you to my parents who still believe in me even when I'm unbearable to be around. Thank you to my brother & sister who dress me up & take me out. Thank you to my suegros who provided me with much-needed childcare & love.

Thank you to Yale University's Windham Campbell Prize for giving me the financial support I needed to create my first-ever office. I could not have finished this book without you. Thank you to the McKnight Foundation for the Junior Faculty Fellowship, which gave me time to finish writing this book in a meaningful way.

Thank you to the late, great Jay Hopler for seeing me & believing in me enough to bring this desert girl to Tampa. Thank you to my students at the University of South Florida, who show me the possibilities of hybrid lenguas beyond Spanglish as a radical means to break English through reimagination. Thank you to Liz Kicak, poet & director of the Humanities Institute, who believed in me when I felt isolated. Thank you to Sonia Ivancic for the comradery in motherhood & academia, a mix that can often feel like oil & water. Thank you to Ajibola Tolase, John Fleming, Thomas Hallock, Diana Leon-Boys, Meredith & Nathan Johnson, Derek Robbins, Julia Koets, Jarod Rosello, Susan Mooney, Alejandro Marquez, & Beatriz Padilla for weathering with me the particular storm that is Florida in the 2020s. Thank you to my department chair, Lauren Arrington, who made space for poetry the minute she arrived in Florida.

Thank you to Dana Levin, my lifeboat in choppy waters, who gave me the word I repeated like a prayer while writing this book: ballast. Thank you to Dan Chiasson for your brilliant mind and support of my work.

Thank you to Ash E. Wynter of Copper Canyon Press for helping me wrangle these poems into shape & for all your thorough notes & patience with me. Thank you to Janeen Armstrong for the generosity of your time & books. & a deep & total thanks to Michael Wiegers who kept asking me for more poems: I kept your notes of encouragement taped to my desk. They kept me going. They kept me alive.

To send these poems out into the world is an affirmation to myself, & hopefully to my readers, that I do still care about living even though I didn't always want to be alive while writing this book (or the last one). I'm only truly alive when I make something every day.

## ABOUT THE AUTHOR

NATALIE SCENTERS-ZAPICO is originally from El Paso, Texas. She is the author of two previous collections of poetry, *Lima :: Limón* (Copper Canyon Press, 2019) & *The Verging Cities* (Center for Literary Publishing, 2015). Winner of Yale University's Windham Campbell Prize, she has held fellowships from the Lannan & Poetry Foundations. She is an assistant professor of poetry & director of the Michael Kuperman Memorial Poetry Library at the University of South Florida. Natalie currently lives in Tampa with her husband, suegros, & young son.

Copper Canyon Press poets are at the center of all our efforts as a nonprofit publisher. Poets create the art of our books, and they read and teach the books we publish. Many are also generous donors who believe in financially supporting the vibrant poetry community of Copper Canyon Press. For decades, our poets have quietly donated their royalties, have contributed their time to our fundraising campaigns, and have made personal donations in support of emerging and established poets. Their generosity has encouraged the innovative risk-taking that sustains and furthers the art form.

The donor-poets who have contributed to the Press since 2023 include:

Jonathan Aaron

Pamela Alexander

Kazim Ali

Ellen Bass

Erin Belieu

Mark Bibbins

Linda Bierds

Sherwin Bitsui

Jaswinder Bolina

Marianne Boruch

Laure-Anne Bosselaar

Cyrus Cassells

Peter Cole and Adina Hoffman

Elizabeth J. Coleman

Shangyang Fang

John Freeman

Forrest Gander

Jenny George

Dan Gerber

Jorie Graham

Roger Greenwald

Robert and Carolyn Hedin

Bob Hicok

Ha Jin

The estate of Jaan Kaplinski

Laura Kasischke

Jennifer L. Knox

Ted Kooser

Stephen Kuusisto

Deborah Landau

Sung-Il Lee

Ben Lerner

Dana Levin

Maurice Manning

Heather McHugh

Jane Miller

Roger Mitchell

Lisa Olstein

Gregory Orr

Eric Pankey

Kevin Prufer

Alicia Rabins

Dean Rader

Paisley Rekdal

James Richardson

Alberto Ríos

David Romtvedt

Sarah Ruhl

Kelli Russell Agodon

Natalie Shapero

Arthur Sze

Yuki Tanaka

Elaine Terranova

Chase Twichell

Ocean Vuong

Connie Wanek

Emily Warn

Poetry is vital to language and living. Since 1972, Copper Canyon Press has published extraordinary poetry from around the world to engage the imaginations and intellects of readers, writers, booksellers, librarians, teachers, students, and donors.

WE ARE GRATEFUL FOR THE MAJOR SUPPORT PROVIDED BY:

academy of
american poets

OFFICE OF ARTS & CULTURE
SEATTLE

ARTSFUND

THE PAUL G. ALLEN
FAMILY FOUNDATION

Hawthornden
Foundation

POETRY
FOUNDATION

INGRAM
CONTENT GROUP

the point
envision·enact·evolve

McSWEENEY'S

WASHINGTON STATE
ARTS COMMISSION

National
Endowment
for the Arts
arts.gov
ART WORKS.

The Witter Bynner Foundation
for Poetry

TO LEARN MORE ABOUT UNDERWRITING
COPPER CANYON PRESS TITLES,
PLEASE CALL 360-385-4925 EXT. 105

## WE ARE GRATEFUL FOR THE MAJOR SUPPORT PROVIDED BY:

Anonymous

Jill Baker and Jeffrey Bishop

Anne and Geoffrey Barker

Mona Baroudi and Patrick
    Whitgrove

Lisha Bian

Rick Shinsui Bowles

John Branch

Diana Broze

John R. Cahill

Sarah J. Cavanaugh

Keith Cowan and Linda Walsh

Peter Currie

Geralyn White Dreyfous

The Evans Family

Mimi Gardner Gates

Claire Gribbin

Gull Industries Inc.
    on behalf of William True

Carolyn and Robert Hedin

David and Jane Hibbard

Bruce S. Kahn

Phil Kovacevich and Eric Wechsler

Eric La Brecque

Maureen Lee and Mark Busto

Ellie Mathews and Carl Youngmann
    as The North Press

Kathryn O'Driscoll

Petunia Charitable Fund and
    advisor Elizabeth Hebert

Suzanne Rapp and Mark Hamilton

Adam and Lynn Rauch

Emily and Dan Raymond

Joseph C. Roberts

Cynthia Sears

Kim and Jeff Seely

Tree Swenson

Julia Sze

Donna Wolf

Jamie Wolf

Barbara and Charles Wright

In honor of C.D. Wright
    from Forrest Gander

Caleb Young as C. Young Creative

The dedicated interns and faithful
    volunteers of Copper Canyon Press

The pressmark for Copper Canyon Press
suggests entrance, connection, and interaction
while holding at its center
an attentive, dynamic space for poetry.

This book is set in Adobe Garamond Pro.
Book design by Gopa & Ted2, Inc.
Printed on archival-quality paper.